FIRE BOY

MY WORRY DOESN'T
FIT ME RIGHT, NOT LIKE THEY
SAY IN CLASS,

SEE IT FEELS LIKE
MY BODY IS MADE OF
FIRE AND MY
WORRIES ARE MADE
OF GAS!

MY WORRY DOES NOT MAKE ME RUN OR
FREEZE
AND
RARELY DOES IT MAKE ME DWELL,
BUT MY WORRY MAKES MY BELLY HOT AND
SOMETIMES THAT CAN SMELL.

I'M ALWAYS KIND OF WARM, AND IT'S TOUGH TO KNOW WHEN,
MY WORRY WILL HEAT ME UP AND I MIGHT
EXPLODE ON A FRIEND!!

THE TRUTH IS, WHEN I DO NOT KNOW
AN ANSWER, OR MAYBE WHAT YOU
MEAN,
I WILL SOMETIMES BLOW UP AND MAKE
AN UGLY SCENE!

SOMETIMES IT WILL HAPPEN IF I'M NOT
SURE HOW TO PLAY OR AFRAID THAT WE
AREN'T FRIENDS,
WORRY CAN STOP BY, AND THAT MY FRIEND
IS THE END!
I BLOW UP LIKE A WILD FIRE
AND YOUR WORDS BECOME LIKE THE WIND,
AND IF YOU'RE TOO CLOSE, YOU MIGHT GET
A LITTLE SINGED.

THERE ARE TIMES WHEN I GET REALLY MAD,
AND I BECOME AN ANGRY CRIER,
BUT CAN YOU REALLLLLLY BLAME A GUY WHEN HIS
BUTT IS LITERALLY ON FIRE!?!!

SO I TRY AND COOL MY BODY DOWN,
A LITTLE ALL DAY LONG,
SOMETIMES I'LL DRINK COOL WATER,
SOMETIMES I'LL HUM A SONG.

I TRY AND GET GOOD SLEEPS
AND LET LAUGHTER IN MY BELLY,
EAT ALL THE GOOD BREAKFASTS AND
LUNCHTIME PB AND JELLIES!

I TAKE DEEP BREATHS,
COUNT MY TOES
OR SQUEEZE MY PALMS A LITTLE
TIGHTER,
OR
I CAN GET MY JOURNAL AND
REMEMBER I CAN BE A WRITER.

MY MOM SAYS MY FIRE IS THERE
TO KEEP ME SAFE AND WARM AND I DO NOT
WANT TO PUT IT OUT,
BUT THAT I WANT TO BE THE BOSS OF IT
AND NOT LET IT CATAPULT!

SO I PRACTICE MY PIZZA BREATHS-
I SMELL THE GOOD SMELL IN AND COOL THAT
HOT SLICE OFF WITH MY BREATH WHILE
COUNTING BACK FROM TWO,
AND REMIND MYSELF,
THAT I KNOW JUST WHAT TO DO!

You got this kid!

9 7 9 8 4 7 5 9 2 6 5 8 1